MW01716268

HIKING OUT OF THE WILDERNESS

Hiking Out of the Wilderness

A True Story of Tragedy, Healing, and Hope from the Ashes

Tamara Lennon

Bookmarked Editorial Services
Los Angeles

Library of Congress Control Number: 2025917096
Hiking Out of the Wilderness: A True Story of Tragedy, Healing, and Hope from the Ashes by Tamara Lennon
Los Angeles, CA: Bookmarked Editorial Services, 2025.

ISBN: 978-1-964399-15-7 (paperback); 978-1-964399-16-4 (Kindle)

Cover Design: Hey Media (itsheymedia.com)
Editing & Layout: Mark Miller

Printed in the United States of America

BOOKMARKED EDITORIAL SERVICES
Los Angeles, CA
www.bookmarkedpages.com

1 2 3 4 5 28 27 26 25

This book is dedicated to my son, Joshua David,
who taught me so much about love and life, forgiveness,
and never giving up hope!

"Love is a safe place of shelter,
for it never stops believing the best for others.
Love never takes failure as defeat,
for it never gives up!"
— 1 Corinthians 13:7 (TPT)

PROLOGUE

Zach Williams wrote a song that pretty much sums up the last twenty years of my life. The lyrics go something like this (in my paraphrased version):

When the voice tells you that you're not enough,
That you don't measure up or have what it takes—
That you're weak, broken, unworthy of love,
That beauty and value are things you'll never carry—
Recognize it for what it is.

Now here is where the title of the song comes in: "*Fear Is a Liar.*" The chorus evokes these general ideas as it continues:

Fear, the great deceiver.
It drains your strength,
halts your progress,
robs your peace,
and suffocates your joy.

But fear doesn't get the final word.
Throw it straight into the fire because…
Fear. Is. A. Liar.

This rings true of my life, especially that fateful day, May 19, 2005. It seems like another lifetime ago, but it was in that moment—when I heard the most horrible news imaginable—that I became paralyzed, immobile, stopped dead in my tracks. And it was in that same moment when life came to a screeching halt that I felt myself floating outside of my body, because not only my mind but even my body couldn't begin to comprehend the most devastating trauma: *Something unthinkable has happened to my adorable, mischievous, beautiful little boy.*

That monster called Fear has bossed me around for far too long, and I'm guilty for believing all of its lies, whether they be small, little lies or entirely exaggerated falsehoods. This enemy of my soul has imprisoned me for years, holding the very key to my captivity. Sometimes when I get a glimpse of him, he is just a little "imp," while at other times, he appears to be a towering monster with big, ugly fangs and an outstretched claw that is ready to destroy me with a single swipe. He then has my full attention—nothing else exists except his whisper: "Whatever you write won't be good enough. It will never be good enough. You will be endlessly writing and editing, always feeling overwhelmed, angry, and frustrated. And if you write about your 'dark night of the soul,' then you will stay stuck there in that bottomless, darkened pit, hopelessly depressed!"

Even now, I cringe at the mere thought of those piercing, vile words. *He's right,* I once told myself. *If I revisit my trauma, then I will have dug myself into a pit with no way of escape.*

But today is a new day, because the Father of Lies cannot make room in my house anymore! In the process of writing this book, I have issued him an Eviction Notice to leave my house—and never to return ever again.

If you have also been tormented by this monster of fear that has tried to make room in your house, please pray this prayer with me:

> *"Lord Jesus, You alone are the King of my heart, house, and soul. I give You permission to evict that demon of fear with all of its minions to never return again! You came to set the captives free, and I thank You for my newfound freedom! Help me, Holy Spirit, my Counselor and Trail Guide, to tread this road to true freedom!"*

It is my hope, prayer, and desire for you to walk in freedom from fear and to know in your heart that it's His desire for you to know true freedom, peace that passes all understanding, and joy that is unquenchable!

"I will say of the Lord, 'He is my refuge and my fortress;
My God, in Him I will trust.'"
— Psalm 91:2

1

TRUE NORTH

My first pregnancy was punctuated by many triumphs and heartbreaks. Regardless of background or social status, I know that countless women can relate to feeling the thrill of entering this new territory of motherhood—where everything in your life changes drastically in so many ways.

You are blazing a new trail that you have never embarked on before, and it is both frightening and altogether wonderful. You spend blissful nights planning all the details in your head: baby names and their meanings, the theme and design of the room, the baby furniture, toys, clothes, and so on. The list can be overwhelming, but you are certain that everything will be absolutely amazing, even if it kills you!

Then as you draw closer to the due date, you begin the "nesting" season where you are feverously cleaning everything from top to bottom, inside and out, including the toilet bowl. You can't explain it—you are suddenly on methamphetamines where you are able to accomplish hours of cleaning without a sweat!

In my moments of "cleaning madness," I was also faced with the heartbreaking reality that my situation wasn't "ideal." It was definitely not ideal for most, and certainly not for someone who identified as a believer. Having a baby out of wedlock as a single mom is often tied to an enormous amount of shame, uncertainty, and fear.

However, when I read the pregnancy test for the second time—because, of course, the first time may have been mistaken—I felt an enormous amount of peace overwhelm me as I surrendered my situation to God, not knowing what the future would hold. Actually, I was very surprised at the extent of grace that I sensed in that moment when my world should have been crashing down.

It was May 2002, and I was at the end of finishing my master's degree at Azusa Pacific University in School Counseling. I was grateful that I had completed most of my coursework and was finishing my thesis. There was an unmistakable whirlwind of activity surrounding me, and I was determined to stay the course, finish all of my requirements, and graduate.

Sharing the news with my parents that I was pregnant was what I looked forward to the least, knowing that I would be shamed by my mom, which was totally to be expected. But a "little bird" had this brilliant idea of initially telling them that they were going to be grandparents, hopefully softening the blow.

When I broke the news, my dad was keen on the idea, but my mother was less than enthused. She immediately barked at me, telling me that she wouldn't be a babysitter. She was clearly angry. Even so, I was relieved that my dad was so forgiving toward me, and he was completely in my corner, supporting me through this process, which was already overwhelming. I've always admired him because he has always been quick to forgive, show compassion, and show a lot less judgment.

There's a quote in *Antony and Cleopatra* by William Shakespeare: "The breaking of so great a thing should make a greater crack."[1] I was definitely in that breaking season of my life where I had the choice to embrace the challenge or run from it. I chose to embrace it and was "all in." With my whole heart, I became completely engrossed in all the preparations for the anticipated birth.

---

[1] Shakespeare, William. *Antony and Cleopatra*. Edited by Barbara A. Mowat and Paul Werstine. New York: Simon & Schuster, 2005.

This was the next stage of my destiny: I was climbing a new mountain, with my past landscape of hills and valleys behind me.

In the movie *Braveheart*, William Wallace proclaims to his fellow men, "Your heart is free. Have the courage to follow it!"[2] On one hand, I felt free, as all of my sins were exposed and nothing was hidden any longer, lending itself to true freedom. Yet, on the other hand, it also required a lot of courage on my part—to move forward into unknown territory as a single mom, not knowing what would happen next, literally.

Several months passed, and I was experiencing bliss. My pregnancy was very easygoing… no morning sickness, weird pains, sleepless nights, or anything like that. The only time I did get really sick was when I accidentally took my prenatal pill on an empty stomach, which didn't entirely agree with me, and I puked all over the interior of my car on my way to work!

In fact, I had so much energy that I started working two jobs; my other part-time job was working seasonal at Macy's in the bedding department. My coworkers, who just so happened to be all the gay guys that worked at that Macy's, would joke that I was going to have the baby right there at work! Fortunately, that never happened, but they were the sweetest guys, always looking out for me. Our

---

[2] *Braveheart*. Directed by Mel Gibson. Los Angeles: Paramount Pictures, 1995.

work environment definitely felt like a sitcom—a single, pregnant woman working with all the gay men on staff at a department store.

One of my most vivid memories while working at Macy's was when "the guys" introduced me to a longtime client of theirs who was a retired nurse. Incidentally, she had worked in delivery at Huntington Memorial Hospital with the very same doctor that was my obstetrician. She shared with me how amazing and wonderful Dr. Lee was with a wealth of experience.

I realized at that moment how much worry I had been carrying about the upcoming birth, but God knew that I needed the reassurance that He had put me into the best hands. During our conversation, I was overcome with so much peace—a peace that transcends all understanding—and I knew in the depth of my being that everything was going to be OK.

It was a warm, beautiful morning in January when I woke up feeling a slight pain in my lower abdomen. I really didn't think much of it, but then as the discomfort steadily grew stronger, I suddenly realized that even though it wasn't February 13, my due date, I was feeling the imminent pains of childbirth.

With a quick holler, my mom and I grabbed everything and headed toward the car. As I stepped outside, I momentarily paused and looked up at the clear, brilliant sky—just to seize that moment, knowing that this day would change my life forever. The sunlight cast an unseasonal splash of warmth across the neighborhood; it really felt like the perfect day.

After that moment passed, we both got into the car and headed straight to the hospital. I remember commenting to my mom, "It's just too warm to be January."

We arrived at Huntington Memorial in no time and parked the car. After hurrying inside and checking in, we walked the long hallway of the hospital with the nurse assigned to me. She was a lovely, blonde lady with long, flowing hair, and her warm smile exuded confidence. "How frequent are your contractions now?" she inquired.

I gave her the numbers but was startled to hear her reply: "Well, it sounds like your contractions are not yet close enough together, so you can go home and come back later."

What?! I didn't know that they were at liberty to tell expectant mothers something like that. After all, I was having contractions and could clearly tell that my baby was coming sooner than later.

I immediately called my friends to begin praying, and literally within ten minutes, my contractions started coming much closer together—on the exact time schedule that the nurse had just explained to me that needed to happen. So, fortunately, I didn't need to make the trek back home. From that minute onward, things began to move like clockwork.

As I was wheeled into the delivery room, I was amazed at how beautiful and adorable the room looked with painted flowers on the walls. Surely, this wasn't a hospital; this was a resort, or as my friends would later share with me, "the Huntington Resort Hospital." And it was every bit of that—with lush greenery surrounding the landscaped gardens. It was truly a joyful experience to give birth at a resort rather than a gray, dismal-looking hospital.

More than just the surroundings, the nurses were just the sweetest, and I was feeling pretty good after the anesthesiologist gave me the epidural. They confirmed that my contractions were now right on schedule, and I had already experienced the worst of birth pangs.

Even though the nurses were doing an absolutely outstanding job tending to me so gently, I had this burning question that I blurted out: "Where is the doctor?" I had heard such wonderful things about him, but he was noticeably MIA!

"Oh, he'll be here soon," one of the nurses reassured me. But still, it just seemed strange that he wasn't yet in the picture, and I automatically found myself visualizing the worst-case scenarios that began swirling around in my head. *What if something happened to him and the backup doctor has to do the delivery? What if…?*

Nevertheless, as my contractions grew much closer—within a couple minutes of each other—the nurse summoned the once elusive Dr. Lee. He came in with a beaming smile as though he had just won the lottery; he wasn't the least bit concerned that he had been MIA in my book! I could have sworn that there were even birds singing as he entered my room.

But now that Dr. Lee was present, it was down to business—the delivery business, that is. He quickly dished out instructions to his taskforce (the nurses) and then looked at me as he gave the orders, "Push as hard as you can! *Push harder*!"

And in that moment, Joshua David was born at 5:14 p.m. Everything about that moment in time seemed so surreal, and before I knew it, there came a bustle of talk and laughter among the nurses.

"Did that just happen?" I asked in a state of happy bewilderment. "Did I just give birth?"

I could hear the voice of my friend in the background quipping, "You didn't suffer enough! Put that baby back in!"

It was true—my labor had only lasted about five hours, tops. My friend and Lamaze partner turned to my dad and said, "You're a grandfather now. How does it feel?"

My dad, with tears welling up in his eyes, was totally overcome with emotion, something that he rarely let others observe. He had always wanted a boy to "roughhouse" and play ball with, someone who would love the game of football as much as he did. It wasn't that he disliked having a daughter—my dad adored me—but having a grandson would be the next best thing to having a son of his own.

As I was wheeled into the postpartum room, I heard the faint sounds of angels rejoicing. Either it was a sensation in my spirit, or the veil between heaven and earth had become very thin. Whatever the case may be, I instinctively knew that there was rejoicing in heaven over the birth of my son. And I believe that is true not only of my son but of every baby that is born, for each child is a precious gift from God. In the midst of this incomparable experience, I was overwhelmed by the amazing revelation of how heaven rejoices over us all!

Fortunately, Mom was way ahead of this impish little man who liked to play games and had a clever response for his amusement: "Josh, thank you for being such a good boy by getting in the bathtub for Mommy!" or "OK, we won't wear clothes today." Those replies usually meant that he wasn't getting the response that he wanted, so he would acquiesce, dip his toe into the bath, but then lay in the tub until *all* of the water went down the drain just in case the tub might fill up again! It's fascinating to wonder, *Where does all that water go once it filters through the drain?*

One of Josh's favorite "loves" was our cat, Mimi, who was not amused by this little, curly-blond-haired boy who smiled sheepishly whenever he came upon her waddling along the hardwood floor. Mimi was our plump, black-and-white-haired cat that Josh so loved with every inch of his being—to the point that he almost burst with inner joy whenever he came upon her. She, however, couldn't seem to care less. She would glide along the side of the bedspread just far enough away so that he couldn't catch her, just out of reach for his little hands. Even so, he would always get so excited because he "almost" caught her in his grasp!

At night, Josh had a routine that he would say goodnight to Papa and Nana, and then after we finished our bedtime prayers, he would say, "Goodnight, Moon! Goodnight, Mimi!" The cat, whether we embraced her pretentious ways or not, was a part of our family, according to Josh.

Besides the infamous word "No!" he had another phrase that he also loved to say especially with Grandma Emma: "The moon is high in the sky!" That was actually the only true sentence that he could express, as he was not yet speaking in full sentences. However, according to Grandma Emma, there were many words that he would speak at her house during his weekly Friday visits that he seemed to forget once Mommy came to pick him up.

Even if Grandma held out a banana and asked, "Josh, what is this?"—which so happened to be his favorite food—he would just clam up if I was present! "What?! Josh, you just said 'banana' for Grandma! You don't want Mom to know that you can say 'banana'?" She would just laugh because everything was a game to him, and it was just more fun to "show off" to Grandma and not let Mom know. He was mischievous, and playing games was an integral part of life!

As we were heading down to San Diego, the "cherub" was fast asleep in his car seat, exhausted and getting some much needed Zs. We finally arrived at our destination two hours later, Campland by the Bay, an expansive RV park situated on Mission Bay. Kids were running around and riding their bikes along the paved paths as we pulled into our campsite, a grassy island located inland from the bay.

There was an older, white bearded man camped next door, sitting on a tree stump and playing his guitar, and Josh was completely captivated by this scene. He would always light up to a melody that was being played. His all-time favorite, the VeggieTales theme song, had to be played while he was consuming his breakfast each morning. If I had forgotten to press play on the CD, he would just sit there, not eating his food, and point to the CD player as if to remind me, "Mom, you forgot that I need music in the morning while I'm eating breakfast!"

We recognized his affinity for music when he was about ten months old. As I picked up Josh after church one day, the Sunday school teacher exclaimed to me, "He lights up when he hears music! None of the other kids have the same reaction as Josh. You can see how much he just loves music!"

So, right when we arrived, Josh heard music playing in the campground and made a beeline for this elderly man with the acoustic guitar. He was so compelled that his little fingers desperately reached out to strum the strings, but the man quickly admonished him to just listen. Obediently, Josh stood there mesmerized.

It was at that very moment, frozen in time, that the Holy Spirit whispered in my ear, "*Something is going to happen to Josh.*"

I immediately sucked in air, trying to breathe as though the wind had been knocked out of me. "What?

That's crazy!" I protested. But that voice was all too familiar. Many questions and doubts flooded my mind: "What's going to happen to Josh? How will it happen? When will it happen? What is *it* anyway?"

As I looked down at my feet, standing there in the midst of grass and dirt, my legs went numb, and I began to feel my heart scream out, "NO!" But it was too late. Those words had already gripped my heart, and there was no turning back.

During the rest of that weekend, we did all of those things that one does while visiting San Diego: enjoying the great outdoors, the sunny beaches, the pleasant campgrounds, and the many sights to see. On the outside, things looked picture-perfect. Yet, on the inside, I desperately tried to forget the agony of those words—"*Something is going to happen to Josh*"—but for the life of me, I just couldn't shake them.

3

THE DREAM

Two short weeks after the spring break camping trip, I would have a dream—the dream that would define me.

In the dream, Josh had left the house with my dad, and I was attending an extravagant party with my mom. This was not your typical holiday party event. A bunch of celebrities and VIP guests were there in attendance, but I somehow knew that they had a nefarious, hidden agenda for this gathering. I began to feel very uncomfortable and convinced my mom that we should leave.

We exited the venue, and just as we were coming around the hedge of a large bush, my dad suddenly met us. I immediately asked him, "Where is Josh?"

My dad replied nonchalantly, "Oh, he's at the metro station…"

I screamed, "*What?* He could have been kidnapped!"

Still inside the dream, my mom and I then rushed to the car, driving north on Lake Avenue in Pasadena as I began to call 911. It was at this very moment that a tow truck screeched through the intersection of Woodbury and Lake, hitting the streetlight head on. The truck driver was flung backwards instead of forwards, which seemed odd at the time, and a young woman stood on top of the truck, yelling for help. The 911 operator came on the line, so I immediately relayed to her information about the accident and said that I was afraid that my son had been possibly kidnapped at the metro station.

As soon as those words left my mouth, I immediately woke up. This was a warning dream, and it absolutely terrified me! Most of the symbolism within that dream was hidden from me at the time. I had awakened to more questions than answers and was in utter disbelief of what I had just witnessed in the dream. My natural response was to pray fervently to God. I also called a close friend, and we talked on the phone late into the night, exchanging thoughts on what that dream might mean.

That next morning, I woke up with a start, realizing that my alarm hadn't gone off. I had inadvertently slept in. So, I hurriedly got ready and explained to my mom to put a chair in front of the French doors that led out to the backyard pool, as just the night before Josh was trying to open them. I had been dyeing my mom's hair in the bathroom when I noticed that he had disappeared, so I quickly ran out to look for him. There he was standing still as a statue just outside of the French doors, looking out toward the backyard. I was in shock, since he had never attempted to open those doors before, and I immediately grabbed his hand, brought him inside, and told him, "Josh, you are not allowed to go outside those doors without Mommy, Papa, or Nana." His response was an emphatic "No!" and he walked away determined that he was going to do what he wanted.

I'd just stood there, shell-shocked, because one thing that I had instilled in him was that we don't say no to adults—otherwise, face the consequences. That was a defining night where he had really crossed the line, and I had witnessed a behavior in him that I hadn't seen before. Questions swirled in my mind: "Why was he so determined to go outside those doors? What possessed him all of a sudden?" I stumbled back into the bathroom where Josh was with my mom to finish the dye job. He clung to her because now the tables were turned and I was the "bad one." Normally, I would have immediately reprimanded him, but for some reason I was silent—and it was not the time to be silent.

So, that following morning, I couldn't seem to shake the feeling of being disoriented as I walked into the kinder classroom, my assignment for that day. On my way to school, I heard the Holy Spirit whisper, "Call your mom and tell her to put the chair in front of the French doors."

"What? I already spoke to her this morning about putting the chair by the door… I really don't think I need to call her," was my reply.

Boy, was I ever wrong! I would go on to regret that decision of not taking those few precious minutes to obey the Holy Spirit that morning during my drive to work—*because that one phone call could have been the call that saved my son's life.* It's crazy to think that a life-and-death decision can be changed in a matter of minutes. And how important it is to obey the whisper of the Holy Spirit even when it doesn't make sense!

Meanwhile, the school day had started, and the children were busy working on their class assignment when the phone rang—the most shocking and horrifying call that I would ever receive. On the other end was a man who introduced himself as a police officer. In an even tone, he proceeded to say, "Ma'am, your son has had an accident in the pool at your house. I've come to drive you to the hospital where they have taken your son."

Immediately I went into shock, my head spinning at light speed as I tried to process the words that I had just heard on the other end of the phone. I was shaken out of my stupor and had the teacher's aide take the class to lunch as I hurried to the front office. In my mind I was hoping that this was just a mistake, that the police officer had accidentally notified the wrong teacher.

Yet, when I walked into the room, the man in uniform looked at me and asked, "Are you Tamara Lennon?" My heart then sank to the darkest, deepest pit—my thoughts had betrayed me, as most assuredly he was looking only for me, because there was no one else by that name.

As we walked outside toward his police car, waves of trauma began to flood over me. He opened the front passenger door for me, and feelings of uncertainty and fear washed over me as I got into the seat of his vehicle. The small realization hit me that I was actually sitting in the front seat of a police car; that alone was traumatic enough.

The officer broke the silence by stating, "Your son has been asking for you." But that was not the case. He must have sensed that I was completely overwhelmed with shock, and he was probably trying to reassure me that my son was okay.

During the ride to the hospital, I dialed the phone number of every prayer warrior I knew. I desperately wanted to cry out, "Start praying!" but my efforts were to no avail as I sickeningly heard one voice recording after another. *How is this possible? No one—not a single person—is answering their phone!*

I would later find out that Janelle, a friend from my small group, had an overwhelming feeling while at work that day—at the very moment of Josh's accident—where she was unable to concentrate, and she instinctively started to pray with a friend. So, even though I hadn't been able to contact a soul, *He* had stirred the hearts of others to begin praying!

The police car pulled up to the entrance of the ER. As I staggered through the front doors of the building, a petite, curly-brown-haired lady met me and told me that she wanted to take me to a separate room to tell me what the plans were for my son. Just as she was sharing her agenda with me, the ER doctor appeared and explained that I, as the mom, had every right to see my son.

As soon as the doctor shared his intention, she immediately began a vehement argument with him. It was utterly bizarre to witness. The doctor gave her a strange look, as even he was taken aback that she would be so indignant. This was just the beginning of the spiritual warfare that I would come up against soon enough.

Fortunately, the doctor won the dispute, and he walked me over to the room where Josh was being held where I recognized a small child, pale under the glaring fluorescent lights, lying motionless on the bed.

The moment I crossed the threshold, a surrealness swirled around me as I hypnotically teetered into the room. But at the same exact moment, I was filled with an unwavering peace. This indescribable sense of peace was present because once I had arrived at the hospital and walked through those automatic doors that led to the ER, I flashbacked to my "911 dream." He had prepared me ahead of time for this very moment. This indescribable peace is depicted in Philippians 4:7, "*And the peace of God, which surpasses all understanding, will guard your hearts and minds through Christ Jesus.*"

In my heart I knew that I had a single purpose as I saw Josh lying there motionless and unresponsive on that hospital bed: to lay my hands over his body and *pray*! I quickly kneeled on the grievous, concrete floor and began to fervently pray in the spirit, as though the Holy Spirit was whispering in my ear, "Just pray because he's going to be OK." The words were slipping out of my mouth as I heard myself pray, "I speak life over you, Josh—*life, life, life*!"

Right then and there, the ER doctor told me in a whispered voice, "Keep speaking life over your son!" What I didn't know and would find out later is that they had been diligently working on Josh for over thirty minutes, and that when I had walked in, they had actually given up—the respiratory therapist with her piercing stare, holding the deflated oxygen bag by her shoulder.

Miraculously, Josh began breathing again. In my vision beyond the veil, Josh was in heaven with Jesus, and it was at that very moment that he explained to my son that he was returning to us because his time on earth was not complete. Seeing the hopeful signs of life, the entire crew pushed him through the long, lingering hallways of the ER and into the stark, infernal elevator.

It didn't seem possible, but we were now heading for the PICU, the Pediatric Intensive Care Unit. There I was introduced to a beautiful woman with long brown hair named Dr. Silva. (I would later find out from my MOPS friend Kelly that Dr. Silva had been her daughter's PICU doctor at Children's Hospital Los Angeles when she had had heart surgery at ten months old. According to Kelly, she was an amazing doctor.) Dr. Silva had the warmest smile, and her presence was the hug that I needed at that very critical moment.

She then explained what their next steps were as a team: to intubate Josh and begin giving him medication intravenously. I was screaming in my head, *Intubate? What does that mean? It sounds so foreign and strange.* I had entered totally unfamiliar territory—the PICU—a place that no parent ever wants to visit because of the horrifying reasons children are brought there.

As Josh lay on the hospital bed with a busy hospital crew of nurses and respiratory therapists working to intubate him, I sat in a chair a formidable distance away and just prayed my heart out. My entire being wanted to be next to him, holding him, and letting him know that everything was going to be OK. Those were the hardest moments as I sat there all alone, without a recognizable soul, save the hospital chaplain praying with me. He then asked me, "Do you want someone from your family to be here with you?"

Well, yes, of course! At his prompting, I called my mom, suddenly wondering where she was in the midst of all this. During the few seconds of waiting for my mom to pick up the call, questions tossed around in my head: *Why wasn't my mom here with Josh in the hospital? He's only two years old, and she's not here with him? What happened?* In my head I was crying out, "*Where are you?*"

My mom came on the line. She explained, between sobs, what had happened that morning from her vantage point. She had been so rattled by the incident that when our neighbor offered to bring her to the hospital, my mom was apparently still in such a state of shock that she just froze up and couldn't make a decision about what to do next.

"How is that possible?" I asked. Not only was this entire experience so unbelievably bizarre and surreal, but my mother's inability to come to the hospital was questionable at the very least. It broke my heart just imagining that Josh had experienced what was definitively the most traumatic event of his life and *no one* was with him—that he had been alone for those forty-five minutes or so. The weighty burden of that thought grieved my soul.

My heart began pounding as the next thought hit me: *Where was my dad?* I then remembered that he had left a few days prior for Gleanings for the Hungry in Dinuba,

CA, which was a good three hours' drive away. Gleanings is a mercy ministry of Youth With A Mission (YWAM) whose mission is to feed the hungry throughout the world, both physically and spiritually. My dad had actually left early to help drive the tractors, as they were planting new crops in the fields. Another wave of devastation hit my heart knowing how crushed he would be to find out that something so terrifying had happened to Josh in his absence.

My inner world began to shift between two of the stages of grief: anger and bargaining.

If my dad had not left early for this mission trip with their Sunday school class, Josh wouldn't have had this accident.

If I had called in sick to work, Josh wouldn't have had this accident.

If I had called my mom on my way to work, Josh wouldn't have had this accident.

If my mom had moved the chair in front of the French doors, Josh wouldn't have had this accident.

It was a tremendous amount of shared guilt. The bottom line was this: We were all to blame for Josh's accident.

I then reasoned through the gravity of my situation further. Since God had given me that prophetic "911 dream," then Josh was going to be OK. He did come back to life and start breathing again after I had prayed for him in the ER room.

God wouldn't have brought him back if He wasn't going to finish what He started, right? He's a God that heals, and we can trust that He is going to fully, completely heal my son. Thus, I had set in my mind that Josh was going to be healed no matter what, just like he had been revived in the ER and all we had to do was pray.

By this time, the waiting room was crowded with people—neighbors who lived on our street, MOPS moms, friends of my parents, and out of the corner of my eye, I recognized a pastor from my parents' church. A little while later, my dad finally arrived, and he was a wreck, barely able to stand on his own two feet. He shared that Pastor Dave had told him what happened to Josh and that they had prayed with him before he left for the hospital. That was the worst drive of his life, without a doubt. My dad related that he actually had to pull over onto the side of the road, as he was overwhelmed by uncontrollable emotion.

"Lord, this is not right!" I prayed. "Why did my dad have to leave early? He wasn't supposed to leave early..." It was obvious that the enemy only wanted to get my dad, Josh's spiritual covering, a far distance away from him so that the enemy would have an "open door" in an attempt to take Josh's very life.

There's a saying, "God is in the details." I can attest to the fact that God was present in the details that fateful day. He certainly knew that this day would come because the Holy Spirit had warned me on our camping trip in San Diego, and He had given me the "911 dream" just the day before. Serendipitously, I would later find out that my friend's cousin, a believer named Lisa, was the very EMT who had responded to the emergency call and was bagging Josh with oxygen and praying over him all the way to Huntington Hospital. Lisa even shared with me that the spiritual warfare was incredible—that on a normal day there is no traffic at that time, but the traffic on Lake Avenue was so busy that they had to take the long way to the hospital.

How is that even possible? Why? There were simply no words that I could muster to express how I felt in those moments. I couldn't understand why there had been such warfare over my son's life. I was furious at the enemy! *Why are you attacking my son? What gave you the legal right?*

As I continued to process everything overloading my reasoning, scenes of my son played across my mind's eye. My dream had always been to have a son, and Josh was the most darling, mischievous little boy who had brought us so much joy! Although he was very strong willed, I had diligently worked with him since he was very young. I had definitive goals as a mom—to be a very informed parent and to make sure that my son knew that he was unconditionally loved and was unequivocally well-mannered. I had read an incredible book, *Growing Kids God's Way* by Gary and Anne Marie Ezzo, which imparted a lot of wise and practical advice in raising kids from a young age, and I implemented most of their ideology into my parenting.

Josh knew basic sign language since he was ten months old—how to sign for "please," "thank you," "more," "yes," and "no, thank you." His mischievous side didn't always want to sign "thank you," but I persisted until he would cave in. He treated it more as a little game and not something that he felt he *always* had to do!

He knew how to pick up his toys and books and help put them away. He knew that there were consequences for whining, throwing a temper tantrum, throwing food on the floor, and saying the word "no" to adults who had asked him to do something. All of my hard work had paid off, as evident in his compliant demeanor. He hardly ever threw a temper tantrum, which was a big deal for a strong-willed two-year-old!

Every Friday when he went to visit Grandma, he would always help her put the toys and books away, and he consistently demonstrated good manners at the table. When Papa and Nana babysat him, he was always helpful and respectful. There were things that he just loved, like VeggieTales, and The Wiggles, and going to Grandma Emma's house on Fridays where they would make cookies together. These were among Josh's most favorite things.

My cherished memories were interrupted when Dr. Silva stepped back into the waiting room. She told us that she wanted to meet with us and give us an update. I don't remember much of anything that she shared except this statement: "Kids are really resilient." Those words resounded in my ears, and they were the very same words that I would cling to.

She had also shared that the next forty-eight hours would be crucial, but in that turbulent period of time, I couldn't even wrap my head around how to calculate how many days that would be. Two days may not be very much time, but when you are involved in a tragic, traumatic accident, time itself seems to unravel in slow-motion.

The next morning I was greeted by the tall, handsome ER doctor who had shared that he was a believer and that his family was praying for Josh. He confessed his astonishment at the prior day's events, as he had never witnessed a patient come back to life before. He shared candidly that he felt Josh would soon just sit up in bed, completely and fully restored to the little boy he had always been.

This encounter gave my heart so much hope to have a personal visit from the ER doctor and to soak in his words, which carried authority. After all, if a doctor believed the impossible for my son, then it must be true!

However, those two days would come and go with very little progress as Josh lay motionless in a medically induced coma. It seemed as if he was imprisoned in his own body, unable to move, but at the same time resting in a deep sleep.

There were times that I would just tell myself, "He's just sleeping, then he'll wake up, sit up, and give me the biggest hug." That's called the denial phase, and it proved to be an effective means of temporarily dealing with a very traumatic accident—because the reality that my beautiful, mischievous little guy was lying in a hospital bed with severe brain damage was too overwhelming to comprehend.

4

"PAPA!"

"Oh yes, you shaped me first inside, then out;
you formed me in my mother's womb…
Body and soul, I am marvelously made!
I worship in adoration—what a creation!
You know me inside and out,
you know every bone in my body;
You know exactly how I was made, bit by bit,
how I was sculpted from nothing into something.
Like an open book, you watched me grow from conception to birth;
all the stages of my life were spread out before you,
The days of my life all prepared
before I'd even lived one day."
— Psalm 139:13-16 (MSG)

During those initial days at Huntington Hospital, I had a lot of time to reflect. This time of waiting was punctuated by time to think about the surreal uncertainty of the present, time to pray about the massive question mark of the future, and time to reminisce on my most cherished boyhood memories of Josh. This waiting pattern was by far the most excruciating of my life.

I was reminded of my "911 dream," where Josh was left waiting at the metro link station, and I was now waiting for what seemed liked an eternity in the waiting room of the hospital. Yet, as I reflected on my beloved son's short life, wonderful memories of his charming personality and boyish wit brought some level of comfort to my heart.

When one becomes a mom, it truly is a new, unchartered territory and such a priceless gift. No bond in human existence is formed that is stronger than that which is shared between a mother and her child. No love so instantaneous, fulfilling, and forgiving.

Motherhood is everything, the vein of your existence. Your heart is forever entwined to that little, precious one. It truly is a calling, one that fulfills your greatest heart's desire. It is the most challenging job that you will ever commit to, and there will be days where you're so sleep deprived that you're convinced you will surely faint at any moment. There will be days where you can't remember the last time you took a shower because your life is now completely consumed with caring for your little one. And to be honest, there were times during that first year where I was pretty convinced that I was just a cow giving milk. That adorable baby boy proved to be so headstrong and very demanding! But that is what I signed up for, and I lovingly acquiesced to his demands.

When going about my daily routine, I would often be stopped by others who would remark how Josh looked like "a cherub," "a little angel" with his blond, swirling curls and big, blue eyes. Grandma Emma was once approached in town by a film crew who wanted to take pictures of Josh, but she shrugged them off. Josh was his own unique, little self and was definitely "all boy." He would rather be outside, riding his scooter or kicking and throwing a ball. Playing outdoors brought him endless joy.

One time when I was talking on the phone to a friend, Josh began running around the house in his diaper while holding a lemon in his tiny fist, completely giddy and laughing throughout the house. That lemon was just another "ball" that he could play with, even though it couldn't bounce. But to Josh, it didn't matter; he had found a new toy. Who knew that a lemon could not only be squeezed to make lemonade, but it could also serve as a toy for a two-year-old boy who was just looking for a new ball to play with?

Those days at Huntington Hospital turned into weeks, and soon we would be moving Josh to a subacute unit for kids. This was all too foreign for me, as I had never heard of a "subacute," let alone one for kids. We had held onto hope that Josh would come home in short order, but that would not be the case. He would remain at that subacute for the next fifteen agonizing months.

It was dreadful being there every day, seeing kids who had similar conditions to Josh with severe brain damage. We heard all kinds of heart-wrenching reasons for their hospitalization: being injured in a car accident, hit by a vehicle while walking in a crosswalk, struck by a car while riding a bike, nearly drowning, and so on. If something can be accurately described as "hell on earth," this place was it for me personally.

During the very first week, I was filled with supernatural hope, believing blindly that Josh would fully recover. A conference was happening that same week at my church, and a pastor by the name of Bill Johnson was speaking. I felt a nudge of the Holy Spirit to go, and in the morning I left the subacute with my parents remaining by Josh's side. I don't recall much of what he shared in his message, but I do remember my heart arising with a newfound hope.

At the end of the sermon, I approached Pastor Bill to share how I was encouraged by his message and then recounted what had happened to my son. His body language shifted as he compassionately listened to my harrowing tragedy, took out a handkerchief, prayed over it, and instructed me to lay it on my son's head. I thanked him for the handkerchief, which I would learn later is often referred to as a "prayer cloth." As I was walking away, I thought to myself, *OK, why did Pastor Bill give me a handkerchief to lay on my son's head? Why would I do that?*

On my way back to the hospital, I was chatting with a friend who explained that praying over a cloth and laying it on the sick was actually biblical. It was even practiced by the early disciples to heal the sick: *"Now God worked unusual miracles by the hands of Paul, so that even handkerchiefs or aprons were brought from his body to the sick, and the diseases left them…"* (Acts 19:11-12).This practice was totally new to me, but I was willing to try anything, even if it seemed odd or strange at the moment.

After I arrived at the subacute hospital, I walked into Josh's room and laid the prayer cloth on his head as my parents watched. I then explained to them how the pastor had prayed over the handkerchief and had told me to lay it on my son's head. My dad was enthused to hear this and continued praying over Josh and talking to him while he rubbed his arms and held his hands.

I stayed there for a while longer, speaking and praying over Josh, until I felt another nudge to go back to the conference for the evening service. Leaving Josh at the subacute was not easy, as it truly pulled at my heart strings, but I had the confidence knowing that my parents would still be there watching over him.

The service ended up going late into the night, so I decided to stay overnight with a dear friend at her place in Pasadena. Early the following morning, I awoke to the light streaming brightly through the large bay window in the living room where I had fallen asleep on the couch. The first thing I did was call my parents to find out how Josh had done the night before.

My dad's voice sounded excited. *What could have happened?* He shared with me that Josh had "awoken" from his coma, turned his head towards my dad, and called out in a loud voice, "Papa!"—the name he affectionately called my dad.

Astounded, I inquired, "Why didn't you call me last night to tell me that Josh had spoken?!"

He fumbled his words explaining that it was so late, just a few minutes before midnight, and that he didn't want to bother me.

"Bother me?" Those words resounded in my spirit. My heart grieved at the very thought: *Josh had spoken, and I wasn't there to hear it!*

Yet, it seemed that God had determined that only my dad would be the privileged one to hear Josh speak, for even my mom didn't hear him call out. Since that fateful morning when I had left for work—and Josh, with crocodile tears in his eyes, said to me, "No, Mommy, don't go!"—I would never hear him speak again. For even though our hearts were filled with hope that God was going to bring complete healing to Josh, it would not turn out the way we had expected. The last thing that Josh would ever say were those words spoken that mysterious night: "Papa!"

I had just walked into Josh's room at the subacute when his respiratory therapist named Karen, a jovial, plump, and warm-hearted woman, ran over to me with the biggest smile on her face. "On my gosh! Josh said a word last night!" she said as she braced my arm.

I was enthralled as she excitedly recounted her perspective of the story: where she was standing when he spoke, how my dad had fallen to his knees in disbelief, and how she had run out the door, proclaiming in a loud voice to the entire hospital staff, "Josh said a word!" Unfortunately, the staff, in turn, didn't believe her, but she knew what she had heard. Without a doubt, a little, curly blond-haired boy had opened his bright blue eyes, turned his head, and in a loud voice cried out, "Papa!"

Karen was beaming, and I was astonished as she detailed her personal account of what had happened that night. It was a moment of celebration as we almost danced right there in Josh's hospital room! In my mind I reasoned, *Well, if he was able to speak a word last night, then surely he will say something today!* And like a kid with great expectation and anticipation, I prayed to God, believing with my whole heart that Josh would awaken again.

However, the minutes grew into hours. *OK*, I thought, *then it's definitely going to happen tonight, just like last night.* As the evening grew near, my heart sank once again. *What if Josh never speaks a word ever again? What if he doesn't get healed? Does God choose to heal some kids and not others?* These questions were weighing heavy on my spirit.

Those days, weeks, and months at the subacute unit of horrors dragged on as I began to wonder if Josh would ever come home. It begged the question, "Is this the kind of place where you check in but never check out?" I had noticed that a majority of the kids there were not going home.

There was Zachary, who had been hit by a car while riding his bike with his friend in the neighborhood. He had a wonderful, loving family who had shared with me that as a boy, Zachary had played USC Trojan Pop Warner football and that legendary football coach Pete Carroll had come to the subacute to visit him and his family.

There was Frank, a teenager who had attempted suicide but was unsuccessful. He had suffered severe brain damage from a lack of oxygen to the brain. He would often pensively look at me, as though he was trying to tell me something, but the words wouldn't ever come out. Just like Josh, he was imprisoned in his own body, unable to communicate his true feelings.

There were many more kids who each had a different story, whose families all shared in the same "club membership." My heart sympathized with all of them in a unique way, as we could relate to one another's experiences on a deeply personal level.

5

FEARLESS ADVOCATE

**Along with other sections of this book, this chapter reflects my personal experience and perceptions during a difficult time in my son's medical journey. Names and identifying details in this section have been changed to protect privacy. The intent is not to assign blame but to highlight the challenges that families can face in complex medical environments.*

Life at the hospital became my new normal. As I adapted further to this medical ecosystem, I was determined not only to advocate for my son but also to champion other children and families walking through similar trauma. My willingness to ask questions and push for answers wasn't always welcomed by others, especially the administrative staff.

In particular, this did not bode well with the Director of Nursing, otherwise known as the "DON." She was a formidable figure and clearly ran things her way, ethical or otherwise. Some staff members defended her experience and praised her competence, but my own interactions with her left me feeling unimpressed, unheard, and extremely unsettled.

After spending several weeks in the hospital and befriending many of the nurses and respiratory therapists, I began to learn more about how the medical field operates, beyond just a superficial understanding. One key observation was that even in the most respected medical settings, mistakes can happen. And they do happen. Doctors are practicing medicine—not perfecting it—and outcomes can be uncertain. Medication errors, for example, are not uncommon, and when patients are fragile, even small missteps can carry serious repercussions. Therefore, the best-case scenario is to have another set of eyes watching at the bed side as much as possible. That reality was sobering, but this was my new normal.

Early on, my intuition told me that something didn't seem right with the charge nurse that was assigned by the DON for the night shifts. The charge nurse is the one supervising the entire ward at a hospital, including all nurses on that floor. He or she usually has a limited number of patients during each shift.

My first step of digging deeper was to investigate the differences between an LVN (Licensed Vocational Nurse) and RN (Registered Nurse). From my understanding, based on my experiences and conversations with trusted contacts in the medical field, certain responsibilities are typically reserved for RNs due to differences in training, scope of practice, and clinical authority.

As I made more observations, the charge nurse in question seemed at times to be someone with an LVN credential rather than an RN credential. When I asked a staff member about it during the night shift, she confirmed that she was an LVN, *not* an RN. That struck me as alarming, and I followed up by meeting with the hospital CEO. While the executive downplayed the situation, I felt compelled to raise the issue, especially considering what I had observed and heard from other families. I insisted that change was needed. Afterward, another medical professional, with whom I had become good friends with, affirmed that this concern had perpetuated for far too long and that speaking up could prompt needed review.

Out of abundant concern, I started documenting my observations and conversations. Other parents respectfully but candidly began sharing their own stories, including one particularly upsetting moment when a mother was reportedly scolded after falling asleep in the waiting room, exhausted and overwhelmed from her child's condition. Stories like that made it clear to me: Families needed an advocate, even if it meant stepping into uncomfortable, formidable territory.

My second inquiry had to do with another charge nurse who worked the night shift, who was a young, red-haired fellow. He seemed to be a competent RN with relevant work experience and a gracious, friendly attitude toward the families. On one occasion, when I asked about the unusual, staggering way in which he walked about, he explained that he had "injured his knee." However, my investigative instincts urged me to pay closer attention.

As with previous concerns, I began speaking with other parents, many of whom had quietly observed things themselves but felt too overwhelmed by their children's condition to act. One father, whose background was in pharmaceuticals, shared that he had witnessed something troubling one night: a blue syringe being withdrawn from a medication cart without clear documentation. He recognized the substance as morphine and questioned the redheaded male nurse directly. Despite a "shifty story" that was given in reply, the matter was never formally reported. You see, many of these parents were just functioning in survival mode after grappling with all the trauma, hopelessness, and inadequate progress of their children.

In light of this, I took it upon myself to report all of my findings to the DON. She was the last person that I wanted to report to, but I had no choice if I wanted things to change. She may not have liked me, but when it came down to our honest conversation, she believed me. As a result, the DON assigned other nurses to keep a watchful eye over the suspected male nurse. Not too long after that, he was confronted by a coworker when she noticed something odd about his behavior. Sure enough, he confessed that he'd had a knee injury and was misappropriately taking morphine from patients and was promptly discharged by the DON.

I had many other "assignments" after that, but the true crowning moment was when the newly appointed hospital administrator requested a meeting with me in his office. This was just a few weeks before Josh would be released. I was nervous and didn't know what to expect as I opened the dark wooden door that led into a beautifully lit, yellow room. The administrator, a short, stocky man, was standing there with the biggest smile on his face. "I just want you to know," he began saying, "that yesterday the DON gave me her resignation letter…"

I almost cried in disbelief! It felt like a victory—not just for me but for every parent who had walked through those doors, carrying more fear and grief than most could imagine. Though many staff members had remained silent, they also seemed relieved. A nurse from that subacute (who would later become one of Josh's primary night nurses when Josh came home) told me that moving forward, only RNs were allowed to serve as the charge nurse on any day or night shift—ending a long-standing concern that had left many of us uneasy.

A line had been drawn in the sand that day. These vulnerable kids would only receive the best of care, and they wouldn't be forgotten or neglected in any way. My heart is happy knowing that during our season there, God used me to help advocate for the most vulnerable kids and to act as a catalyst for positive change. After all, every precious life, every child, was worth it.

6

AN OCTOBER HOMECOMING

It was a bittersweet homecoming. After more than a year had passed by, I was overcome with feelings of frustration and pure anger that it had taken this long for Josh to be discharged. Never in my wildest dreams did I think that it would take fifteen months to come home from that "subacute of horrors." I didn't know whether I should cry my eyes out in utter disbelief that the day had finally come or just drive that bitter sword deeper into my heart.

Those fifteen months had been grueling—heartbreaking, and utterly exhausting! But I can look back and see God's faithfulness through it all! My dear friend Connie faithfully came to visit every week, encouraging me, praying with me, and sometimes just sitting with me during this long tumultuous winter season. I had also made friends with several nurses, respiratory therapists, and physical therapists, who taught me so much about the medical field.

Truth be told, God had given me the supernatural strength and endurance to face what would be considered by many to be impossible. I experienced firsthand how His strength overcomes our weakness, even our greatest weakness in our darkest days. It was a surreal time, but I knew I had to stay strong for my son.

I vividly remember that pivotal meeting where we had gathered to discuss the protocols for taking Josh home. Ronald, the subacute hospital administrator, sat in his brown leather chair across from me with a big smile on his face, sharing the specifics as to what would be required before Josh could leave the premises. I had to perform a three-day trial run with a friend where we would take over full-time care of Josh—administering his medications, nebulizer treatments, baths, physical therapies, and so forth. It was an intense regimen, but I knew that I could do it and prove to everyone at the subacute hospital that my son had earned the right to come home.

Despite the positive prospects ahead, I was angry at God. *Why did we have to wait so long for Josh to come home? Why didn't You expedite his homecoming?* These questions stirred in my heart along with many others. It seemed incredibly unfair. *After all, You allowed Josh to have this tragic accident!*

That final complaint echoed in my soul, but I wouldn't stay around long enough to listen to His reply because I couldn't bear to hear another disappointing answer.

I was still carrying the weight of the disillusionment that hit me fifteen months prior. When the first doctor at Huntington Memorial had told me in no uncertain terms that Josh wouldn't be able to come home, he specified that he himself wouldn't have been able to do the required care if Josh were his son, and consequently, the only alternative would be to have him transferred to a subacute hospital. It was at this moment that everything inside me just broke. It was unbearable to hear that news, and I seethed with anger at the unjust situation.

Now, over 450 days later, the silver lining in all of this was that Josh was coming home on my dad's birthday, October 8. Josh adored my dad and fondly called him "Papa." His homecoming was the best birthday gift that my dad could have ever received.

To help with Josh's at-home care, I recruited two amazing nurses, Marcos and Diana. Both of them were significant blessings because I already knew them well and could testify that they were highly competent, loyal, and trustworthy. It brought delight to my heart that at least two of Josh's nurses would not be strangers! We definitely had our share of wacky individuals who were assigned to care for Josh. Some nurses would be no-shows, which meant that I had to do a double shift, spending the night in a sleeping bag on the floor in Josh's room and administering his medications throughout the night.

My cousin Sherri gave me some good advice to hone my perspective: "These nurses are not your friends. Treat it like a business—because they work for you!" My heart wanted to become friends with all of them just like when Josh was in the hospital, but now things were decidedly different. We were home, and I was the one calling the shots. In that space the Holy Spirit was faithful to give me discernment regarding which nurses I could trust and which ones I couldn't.

Even with our ups and downs, the home health agency had assigned some great nurses who had a big heart for Josh. Nestor and Winnie stood out due to their faithfulness and loyalty that they showed Josh until the very end.

Nestor was an exceptional nurse who had such compassion for kids, always acted professionally, and was dependable with a family of his own. (I am still friends with his wife, Cristina, who reaches out every so often.)

Then there was Winnie, a full-figured, African American woman, who was our biggest blessing and answer to prayer. She had the biggest heart, and she loved Josh well. My family members and I stay in contact with her to this day and frequently get together with her during the holiday season.

Before his accident, Josh naturally had an incredible connection with African Americans at such a young age. He adored Nicole, a staff member at the Walter Hoving Home who had long, beautiful braids so much that he didn't want to leave when Mom told him it was time to go. He'd just give me a certain look as if to say, "This is my *other mama*, and I'm not ready to leave yet!"

His best friend at two years old was Kai, who was half Korean and half black. Josh would be seated in his car seat next to Kai in the back of the car and jovially call out his name, "Kai, Kai, Kai..." He would then be so thrilled to have Kai sitting next to him in the same car on whatever adventure that we were embarking on. When Kai came over to visit, Josh would stand at the gate, calling out his name and jumping up and down. It was adorable. His little heart loved Kai so much.

Once, when we were at Grandma Emma and Grandpa Brian's house for a backyard fundraiser party, Josh made a beeline for a little African American girl dressed in pink with a matching bow in her hair. He immediately jumped up onto her dad's lap and gave her the sweetest hug. It's true: Kids are color blind. They simply love everyone regardless of the color of their skin. And that's who Josh was—he loved everyone, no matter their appearance.

We have so much to learn from kids. In my own journey with Josh, he taught me so much about life and love. That was his biggest gift to me!

My deepest desire as a mom was that he would know in his heart of hearts how much he truly was loved. If there ever was a time where he got "off track," there would be definite consequences, but I would also explain to him what Mommy's expectations were and pray with him. Not a day went by that I didn't tell Josh how much I loved him. Every single day I told him how much he was cherished and loved. I would always pray over him each night as I put him to bed. And it was clear that he knew in his heart how much he was loved—by Mom, Papa, Nana, Grandma Emma, Grandpa Brian, and Stuart, their special-needs son who lived with them.

Stuart, for his part, had an amazing heart for Josh. Although Stuart could not share his thoughts or feelings because of his disability, one could feel the love he had for Josh. Stuart was in the habit of asking Emma, "Mom, when is Josh coming over?" Even though he knew the schedule that Josh would always come on Fridays, he always wanted to make sure.

Stuart was the de facto supervisor, standing against the doorpost, keeping a watchful eye on that mischievous little guy. If Josh ever was getting into something that he wasn't supposed to be touching, like the cute figurines displayed on the table, Stuart would holler, "Mom! Josh!"

Emma would then come running over and exclaim, "Joshua! What are you doing?"

At that, a smirk spread across Stuart's face, knowing he had fulfilled his job assignment as "toddler supervisor."

Because Stuart was on the autistic spectrum, he normally didn't want anyone to hug him, but Josh, unashamedly, would crawl up onto Stuart's lap and give him the biggest hug. It was absolutely adorable! At first, Stuart protested, but he finally gave in to Josh's charming persistence. Josh had won over his heart, and that was exactly what Stuart needed—a child who would love him unconditionally, regardless of his disability. We have a lot to learn from the littlest ones about how to love without restrictions.

Stuart loved the walks that they would take every Friday with Josh to the school playground. They would slide down the slide together, two kids having the time of their lives. That playground was a special place, where they both laughed and frolicked. As adults we have largely forgotten the importance of play, but our kids remind us how soul nurturing it is to engage in it.

Probably one of Josh's favorite Friday activities with Grandma Emma was baking homemade cookies together. Stuart loved watching Josh have so much fun, gleefully stirring the cookie dough and tasting it. They all enjoyed the final product, warm and gooey chocolate chip cookies that Grandma and Josh had made, with Stuart again serving as "toddler supervisor."

The two boys had a lot of fun and shared memories that bonded them together. When Josh had his accident, Stuart was devastated. He couldn't express his emotions, so he would run out of class and into the street, not really knowing how to grasp the overwhelming feelings of loss. He then would insist, "Mom, pray for Josh!" The little boy who had captured Stuart's heart was lying in a hospital bed for the longest time—imprisoned in his own body.

We now had an arduous road ahead of us with numerous alternative therapies, which were very costly. Along the way, Grandma Emma had a brilliant idea to do a fundraiser to raise money for Josh. Grandpa Brian, who was an amazing chef, would cook the appetizers, their dear friend Eddie would play bartender to serve drinks, and then we would ask for donations from small businesses to support our silent auction. We would make all of the baskets ourselves and then ask any friends who were interested to donate a basket as well. We would also hire a music performer for the event.

Our inaugural fundraiser was a great success, and we raised $3,000. This was exciting to see after all our hard work, and we knew that we could raise so much more the following year.

Emma's best friend, Carmen, lived across the street and donated her beautiful back yard for the event. She helped us organize and assemble all of the exquisite silent auction baskets. We then created beautiful invitations and sent them to everyone we knew. The food was amazing, and the baskets looked beautiful, as Emma had extensive experience in design and in retail as a manager. Their friend John, a true entertainer, was our MC for the event and always made it wonderfully fun for everyone who attended.

The following year, we raised almost double what we had raised the first time around. We continued our fundraising events for the next two years, and we were amazed by the outpouring of love and support from friends, family, and even total strangers who had heard about Josh's accident and our annual silent auction event.

Meanwhile, our alternative therapies included hyperbaric treatments, where I would go inside of a hyperbaric oxygen chamber (which looked much like a mini submarine) with Josh for about an hour. We had a total of forty sessions, which cost about $4,000. Although I had never heard of hyperbaric treatments before, they proved to be immensely helpful for Josh, who had suffered brain hypoxia, or severe brain damage from a lack of oxygen. There is never a guarantee if hyperbaric oxygen treatments will prove to bring about lasting changes, but we had nothing to lose. Based on my research and interviews of other parents who had used the treatments, I felt that the minimum would be that his seizures would be reduced and that he would no longer have to take three different types of seizure medications. We did see improvements, as his relentless seizures dramatically declined, and we were able to wean him off two of his seizure meds and even reduce his other medications.

Up until this time, Josh had been experiencing seizures lasting for forty-five minutes on average, and he would have to be rushed to the ER just so they could sedate him. Earlier on, when he had been admitted to the subacute for the first few weeks, he had one of these seizure episodes, and we had him rushed by ambulance to another local hospital. As the days spun by, I lost count of how many times I rode in the ambulance to take Josh to the hospital.

It was during one of the ER visits that I encountered a physician who insisted that there was no room for Josh in the PICU and that there was nothing he could do. But I had met this doctor before and was already familiar with his dismissive manner. I challenged his response, explaining that according to Josh's pediatric neurologist, there were still additional treatment options available—seizure medications that hadn't yet been tried. He stood there motionless, stone-faced, without a word in reply. After a pause, he finally said he would look to see if there was a bed available.

Later, after we had returned to the subacute, I learned from one of the staff members that it was likely the doctor had been reluctant to admit Josh because of the paperwork involved—not because of a true lack of space. In fact, at that time, only one other child was being treated in the unit. The physician had left the room curtly, followed closely by his younger resident colleague. My mother, who had witnessed the entire exchange, sat in stunned silence before saying, "Wow—I can't believe he talked to you that way!"

I knew I had stood my ground. I may have felt intimidated during our first encounter, but this time, I was resolved not to back down. On our final day in the PICU, the charge nurse discretely shared with me that if I wanted to file a written report about the incident, I had the right to do so. "You're not the first parent to raise concerns," she said. "Others have as well."

But I uncharacteristically declined. I was emotionally spent, physically exhausted, and knew deep inside that God would take care of this situation on my behalf (Deuteronomy 32:35).

7

A FINAL FAREWELL

In the book *Embraced by the Light*, Betty J. Eadie describes in detail the personal encounter she had in heaven after her near-death experience in 1973. More than anything else, this book imparts the hope and expectancy that our loved ones who have gone before us know that it will only be a matter of time before they see us again! Through stories like these and especially the Scriptures, our faith can be strengthened by this truth: "*For now we see but a faint reflection of riddles and mysteries as though reflected in a mirror, but one day we will see face to face…*" (1 Corinthians 13:12, TPT).

Fast forward to August 2009, when I had another dream encounter—a prophetic dream that left me mystified. In the dream I was staying overnight with my friend Rebecca, and I received a phone call from my mom. Her voice urgently relayed that they had to call 911 because Josh was having breathing issues, and he had been rushed to White Memorial Hospital. This seemed odd to me, as White Memorial was located in the Boyle Heights area of Los Angeles where my father had grown up, and that was nowhere near Pasadena, where my parents lived.

Nevertheless, the dream continued as Rebecca dropped me off at the front door of the hospital. In my mind I had a premonition: *This could be life or death for Josh.* The moment I crossed the threshold and stepped into the hospital foyer, I felt as though I had time traveled to the past.

As I scoped the hospital foyer, I noticed that the nurses were all wearing starched white uniform dresses, white rubber-soled shoes, and stiff, white hats. They were treading on a deep red carpet, and the building had wooden architectural features that intrigued me as I looked around.

One of the starched-clad nurses recognized me and walked over to report, "You have a message from the doctor on the phone. He will meet with you, and the Comforter will be there as well."

An immediate thought permeated my mind: *That is a very strange name for a nurse!* As I was processing what the nurse had just shared with me, I then ventured to pick up the smooth, blackened antique rotary phone receiver and listened to the doctor's message.

At that, I immediately woke up from my dream. I sat up in bed bewildered, trying to make sense of this surreal encounter. What I would learn later is that my Aunt Betty, my father's beloved sister, had passed away many years ago from a brain aneurysm at White Memorial Hospital.

In the moment, however, my heart's cry was, "Lord, what are You trying to tell me in all of this? Are You trying to prepare me, just like You did with the '911 dream,' that You are now calling Josh home?"

I began to bargain with God: "If You are going to take my son, then who is going to watch over him? Everyone that he knows is here on earth, and he will not even have a grandparent to take care of him! He's a child, after all, and he can't be left to fend for himself!"

That was what I earnestly told Him, the Creator who bestows life and breath upon all the living. These were my grievous proclamations, wrapped tightly around my aching heart that could find no solace. But He had another plan—a much better plan than I could ever imagine.

Several months passed after I had that fateful dream. It was now May 2010, the month when both Mother's

Day and my mom's birthday would be celebrated. But I had a reason to dread that month: May 19 had been set in stone as the day of Josh's accident—making me wish May never even existed.

On this particular morning, I woke up early and quickly perceived that something wasn't right. Josh's oxygen saturation levels were low, and whatever I attempted to do wouldn't increase his numbers. There was nothing left to do but call 911.

When we were finally settled in the ER, I gazed at the nurse across the from Josh's bed and noticed her name tag: *Gloria.* She had a very sweet disposition as she began to share with me, "All the children in the choir at my church have been singing that song about Joshua who fought the battle of Jericho."

I was taken aback. In the moment I could tell that the Lord had a significant message for me and that this was not a mere coincidence.

Later, as I was wandering the halls during the shift change of nurses, I suddenly ran into Gloria again. "Thank you for all of your encouraging words," I told her. "They mean so much to me!" Then I hugged her, and as I was stepping back, I heard Him whisper in my ear, "You're going to see My glory!"

It was then that the strong realization crashed over me: *Josh will not be coming home.* My soul started treading the emotional depths surging around me. "How could this be?" I prayed. "What are You trying to tell me?" But I didn't really want to hear the answer that I already knew in the depths of my heart.

Josh was in the PICU, the one that I was all too familiar with from the weeks that we had spent there initially. I looked down at my phone and noticed the date staring back at me, taking on a life of its own. *May 18*—the day before the anniversary of Josh's near drowning accident.

Time lapsed, and I was awoken suddenly by the PICU doctor. The face of my phone showed 2 a.m. With a serious tone of voice, he began to tell me something very urgent: "Honestly, I never thought I would be telling you this, but I received the results from the CT scan, and your son has severe sepsis. All of his organs are shutting down—there is nothing that we can do to help him. I'm so sorry."

The ache in my heart grew ten times bigger, instantly throbbing in anguish. Yet, paradoxically, at the same time I felt this unexplainable peace—a peace that surpassed all understanding—as though I was wrapped in His wonderful presence. It was the Comforter!

As the doctor met with me and unloaded the horrible verdict, the Holy Spirit, my Comforter, was with me. Even though my parents and friends had already gone home several hours prior, I was not alone. I felt the reality of what Jesus promised in John 14:16, "*And I will pray the*

Father, and He will give you another Helper, that He may abide with you forever."

Then the remembrance of that dream came flooding back, along with the nurse's instruction: "The doctor will meet with you, and the Comforter will be with you!" It had been more than nine months since, but this meeting with the doctor seemed to play out just like my dream had foreshadowed.

Later that morning, Shelly and Ann Tubbs, a pastor from our church, met me at the hospital. Ann brought her keyboard along, and we had a time of worship together in Josh's room while he lay in bed. Afterward, Ann shared with me a vision that she had during worship: "I saw Josh standing next to Jesus, and He was giving him a choice—to be with Him in heaven or to stay with us here on earth."

My heart began to melt. I immediately knew that the vision I had just received during our worship time was the second part of her vision. In my mind's eye I saw Josh standing near the "sea of glass" where about fifty or so children around his age had gathered. They were all shouting out his name, jumping up and down, so excited to meet him. My heart could hear their resounding voices: "Josh! Josh!"

The most surreal part of this vision was that I could personally feel the genuine love that these children had for my son. It truly was an unbelievable feeling of comfort. It gave me so much peace to know that Josh would have friends to play with—he wouldn't be abandoned or alone. Standing on the perimeter were angels dressed in white robes, with their hands folded silently as they looked on. Thus, I knew in my heart that Josh had made his choice, and it was up to me to accept it.

Before that day, I had experienced other visions of heaven, where I had seen the same sea of glass, but never so vividly. The biblical reference for this is found in Revelation 4:6, which states, "*Before the throne there was a sea of glass, like crystal…*" My heart was immensely comforted knowing that my son had chosen to be with Jesus and all those new little friends that were waiting for him in heaven. Even still, a question lingered in my soul: *If Josh were to transition to his heavenly home, who would look after my son?*

The very next day would be Josh's last day with us. As we gathered around his hospital bed—Grandma Emma, my parents, and myself—we only had a few hours left with him before his passing from this earthly life to his new eternal home. We cherished this time talking to Josh, singing to him, and just loving on him in his very last moments with us.

He quickly passed away soon after he was taken off all life support. It happened so suddenly that I wasn't really prepared for it. Despite the abrupt nature of his passing, my heart rejoiced that my son, who had suffered such a traumatic accident, no longer was suffering in his earthly body. He now had a new body and was in a place where he could run and jump and play—and be the boy he was created to be. He now had his new friends in heaven to celebrate his true "homecoming."

The following day, I had an overwhelming feeling that I couldn't explain, but there was a knowing in my heart that my Aunt Betty—my dad's older sister who looked after him and his brother while they were growing up—was now a "surrogate grandmother" to Josh. She would be the one designated to watch over him in his new heavenly home. And even though she had passed away at a young age, a year before I was born, I also felt that I somehow "knew" her, in spite of the fact that we never had the chance to meet.

My heart was filled with an overwhelming peace knowing that Josh had someone to look after him, someone to love him with all their heart in the same way that we loved him. I pondered all of these things internally, not exactly sure how to explain what I was feeling to others. Truth be told, I had never heard of anyone having this "heavenly epiphany" before, to realize that a family member whom you never had met is now looking after your child just as a loving grandmother would. And to take it beyond my wildest expectations, I had the strongest feeling that I knew her in my heart and that she would take good care of my son, my beloved son.

But, true to His nature as a devoted Father, God always gives us relevant "prophetic signs" just to let us know that we're not completely hallucinating or fabricating these spiritual realities. One day later, my dad had a dream. In the dream he was sitting in his famous, wooden rocking chair, and his sister Betty approached him, put her arm around him, and said, "Don't worry. He's with me." It was clear to my dad that she was speaking about Josh.

When he told me this significant dream, I immediately knew that it was total confirmation of what I bore witness to in my heart! That reassuring dream was what my dad so desperately needed—a peace knowing that Josh was well taken care of by Aunt Betty now that he was no longer with us here on earth.

The day had come for my cherished, beloved son's funeral. We had a plot picked out at Forest Lawn Glendale where most of my dad's family is buried, including Aunt Betty.

We had a wonderful service at the "Wee Kirk O' the Heather" church led by Pastor Dave, my former youth pastor. I had chosen an adorable picture of Josh with the biggest smile on his face holding a baseball as the cover for the program with the following scripture:

"No man will be able to stand before you, Joshua,
all the days of your life.
Just as I have been with Moses, I will be with you;
I will not fail your or forsake you."
—Joshua 1:5

My cousins Sherri and Dean Edwards had created a beautiful video memorial set to music with all of the wonderful memories we had of Josh as a family. We then ventured out to the burial spot, *Everlasting Love*, where we sang worship songs led by Kenny Peavey, our worship pastor, and then released balloons with a message to Josh at the end of the service.

I am convinced that Josh was among his friends in heaven laughing and catching the balloons! My Aunt Carol, Aunt Betty's daughter, later shared with me after the service that she had seen her dad standing next to the very tree that I had previously seen Josh standing by holding a leaf just days before. There's a verse in Proverbs that exemplifies how God is in the details of our lives: *"In all your ways acknowledge Him, and He shall direct your paths"* (Proverbs 3:6).

The ensuing days felt lifeless. My central identity as Josh's mom had become nonexistent. An endless barrage of questions bombarded me: "Who am I if I am no longer

Josh's mom? If there's no one to call me Mom, does that mean I'm no longer a mom? How do I respond to those who ask me if I have any kids? Is it possible to be a mom one day, then the next day your entire significance as a mom is erased?"

The beautiful truth is that the Lord knows how to comfort our hearts in the midst of unbearable loss.

Even with so many questions and uncertainties, I tenaciously held onto the words that God had given me in my heart. I reminded myself of the vision and the dream that I'd had, and no one could take them away from me.

Never in your wildest dreams do you ever believe that your child will not only have a life-altering accident but will then pass away five short years later. It is overwhelming, heartbreaking, and unbelievable all at the same time.

If there ever was a "dark night of the soul," that season of my life was undeniably it! I had lived in perpetual survival mode for so long that I didn't really know how to live a "normal life." There was nothing normal about my life anymore.

Again and again, I returned to the words graciously provided by my Heavenly Father. I held onto the word that my Aunt Betty, a survivor and advocate in the truest sense, would be like a grandmother to my son, taking good care of him and watching over him in heaven. And with a sense of divine assurance in my heart, I could dredge through the wilderness of the journey before me—a journey into the "great unknown."

Hebrews 12:1 became a living reality for me: "*Therefore we also, since we are surrounded by so great a cloud of witnesses, let us lay aside every weight, and the sin which so easily ensnares us, and let us run with endurance the race that is set before us.*"

With the Comforter as my trail guide, I would learn to brave the most perilous trails and cliffs. Sometimes along the way, I find myself blindsided by grief, frozen in time and unable to move. Other times I am smacked by a memory from the past that creeps up and haunts me during the day, gripping my heart strings with the thought that there isn't a single thing I can do to bring my son back.

Then there are other times where I have a fleeting thought, a sweet, heavenly picture or vision of him running in a field, laughing, and playing with other kids.

There have been times where I've felt as if I had one foot permanently placed secured on earth and another behind the veil, in an otherworldly reality.

It was as though I was given a key, an ancient key to unlock the heavenly realm that reminded me very much of Narnia.

I could envision rolling hills, beautiful horses galloping freely, children racing and giggling with joy, birds singing, and the most beautiful symphony resounding throughout the land.

Every aspect of creation was playing its own harmonious composition.

And in these sacred moments of solace, it is as though I am alone with my Creator, caught up in this symphony, basking in the beauty of everything that His hands have created.

I am swept up by the beauty and reminded that my son is in a far more glorious, heavenly home, where he is loved and cherished, not only by my Aunt Betty but by my parents, his true grandparents, Papa and Nana.

8

HEAVEN IS FOR REAL

In the years since Josh's heavenly homecoming, I am so grateful for all of the amazing prayers, love, and support that I received during this very difficult and traumatic journey. I'm reminded of the amazing MOPS moms who poured out their heartfelt care, sacrificial time, and generosity during those perilous first weeks at the hospital. They provided an abundance of dinners for my family and attended each and every silent auction fundraiser we organized for Josh.

My most vivid memory is of Marcy, camping out in the hospital waiting room with a journal so that all the mothers who came to visit could write me an encouraging prayer or note letting me know that they were thinking of me, so that I could spend my devoted time by Josh's bedside.

Another memory in the infamous waiting room was a visit from Michelle, another MOPS mom who was a licensed therapist. Michelle shared with me some enlightened wisdom: that people react in very strange ways when dealing with trauma, and to be careful who I surround myself with during this time.

Her wise advice has proven to be true time and time again, as I have witnessed some of the most unbelievable reactions and responses from friends, family, and hospital staff. Trauma is a strange animal that can take on a life of its own if not handled with care. Once you're infected by it, it doesn't simply go away. It lingers in the darkest corners and rears its ugly head when triggered, very much like a wild animal does when confronted.

Memories come back to me of the wonderful support groups that I joined for grieving parents at Glendale Adventist Hospital and the parents I met there. It was at this hospital that I would meet Alice, a wonderful grief counselor, hospital chaplain, celebrated speaker, and friend. I joined every small group and grief training that she led. Her teachings and pearls of wisdom were like water to my thirsty soul. In her I had found an amazingly compassionate counselor who helped me navigate the most perilous trails of my arduous journey out of the wilderness.

Throughout Josh's hospital stay, there was one scripture that kept coming up time and time again: Psalm 91. A mother who had been in the PICU with me those first few weeks shared with me that she had heard my story about Josh's accident and told me to declare Psalm 91 over my son. The following verses brought me great comfort: *"He who dwells in the secret place of the Most High shall abide under the shadow of the Almighty. I will say of the Lord, 'He is my refuge and my fortress; my God, in Him I will trust'"* (verses 1-2).

I had another divine encounter when my friend Amy's father, Jerry, called me from Colorado those first few days in the PICU. He shared the following verse from Isaiah with me and instructed me to speak it over my son. He also prophetically shared with me how the enemy will also try to stir up counterfeit solutions that are contrary to trusting in the Lord.

> *"When you pass through the waters, I will be with you; and through the rivers, they shall not overflow you. When you walk through the fire, you shall not be burned, Nor shall the flame scorch you"* (Isaiah 43:2).

There are many books that I have read on grief, but only a few were ones that I truly resonated with: *Embraced by the Light* by Betty J. Eadie, and *Heaven Is for Real* by Todd Burpo (which later was made into a wonderful movie). Both of these books gave me great comfort as well as confirmation of the many prophetic dreams and visions that I've had.

In the true-life story of three-year-old Colton Burpo, he shares quite candidly with his parents how Jesus had given him homework. This retelling of his experience in heaven confirmed the dreams that I'd had after Josh passed away. In one dream I was visiting Josh in heaven, and he was showing me his "classroom" where he was learning all about dinosaurs.

Colton also shared that one of the things that he missed after visiting heaven was "playing with lions."[3] This made me laugh because I also had a dream of an expansive, beautiful pool in heaven, and Josh and all of his friends were sliding down the tail and body of a killer whale, which had the biggest grin on its face—as though it was overcome with joy that all of these kids were having the time of their life.

Moreover, I had known in my heart that my Aunt Betty was looking after Josh, but it became even more real when Colton said that he had met his great-grandfather in heaven whom he affectionately called "Pop." He shared, "It was cool because in heaven if I wasn't with Jesus, I was with Pop and he was taking care of me."[4] Just

---

[3] "Heaven is For Real with Colton Burpo," Impact Podcast with John Shegerian, December 22, 2020, https://impactpodcast.com/episode/2020/12/heaven-is-for-real-with-colton-burpo/
[4] Ibid.

as Pop was helping to take care of Colton, Aunt Betty was taking care of Josh.

Colton also explained, "So it's really cool because family is still a really big thing in heaven."[5] This really made me smile—every dream and vision that my dad and I had experienced was confirmed through this little boy's recounting of heaven.

Colton fondly shared how when he was undergoing surgery, he was sitting on Jesus' lap, and Jesus had asked the angels to sing some of his favorite songs, like *Joshua Fought the Battle of Jericho.* This rings true for Josh's story. When Josh had undergone a tracheotomy surgery in the first week of his accident, I knew in my heart that Jesus was with him and was singing over him some of his favorite songs as well!

"Heaven," according to Colton, "feels like home because you finally get to be with God."[6] This comforts my heart knowing that Josh is living his best life in his real home with friends, family, and most of all, his Creator. Heaven is a perfect home where he is in the presence of the Lord, in constant fellowship with God.

---

[5] Ibid.

[6] Ibid.

9

WILD FIRE

No one gets through this journey of life without difficulties and challenges, trauma and losses. As for me, I was totally unaware that I would be facing another tragic loss, and the only clue that I had was the same "warning angel" that had visited me in a dream the eve before my mom's tragic fall.

It was the beginning of January 2025, just days before I was set to return to school after winter break. I had just come home from running errands and crossed the threshold of the back door into the kitchen when, out of nowhere, I was struck by a flash of a picture—a vision—of a man sitting silently in the breakfast nook. But this was no ordinary man, for I recognized him from a previous dream that I had a few years before on November 23, 2021.

At that time, my mom and I flew out to Texas to spend my Thanksgiving break with family since my dad had passed away in October of 2020. In my dream that night in 2021, I was in a nondescript bedroom, conversing with a friend, when I noticed that a man dressed in a suit suddenly appeared at the threshold of the door. He just stood there without saying a word to us. My immediate reaction was to scream out, "No!" It was so intense that my physical body was actually attempting to scream at that moment, which jolted me awake.

I felt perplexed, completely in the dark as to what that dream meant. I'd had various forms of vivid, prophetic dreams, but this dream was different. The man, probably an angel, stood before me in total silence, and in my spirit I knew that he had come with a warning.

Sure enough, later that day, my mom had a traumatic accident where she fell and fractured her hip. As a result, she needed to undergo partial hip replacement surgery the very next day, Thanksgiving Day.

What struck me even more in hindsight were the parallels between that dream and the vision I had on this January afternoon in 2025. In the dream, the man stood at the threshold of the doorway. In this vision, I had just physically crossed the threshold into the kitchen when I saw him again—this time seated at the breakfast nook, with one leg propped up, dressed almost identically, and still completely silent. The symbolism wasn't lost on me. Spiritually, thresholds often mark a place of transition, where one season ends and another begins. It's a crossing point, a liminal space where change unfolds and unseen realities break through.

In many biblical and spiritual traditions, thresholds are seen as sacred spaces—where heaven brushes against earth and divine messages are delivered. The Bible alludes to this in Ezekiel 10:18: "*Then the glory of the Lord departed from the threshold of the temple…*"

Different rooms in one's house can also have prophetic significance. The kitchen is considered the place of nourishment, hospitality, and provision, symbolizing a space where God wants to prepare, provide, and sustain us by His grace. Kitchens can also indicate things that are being made ready or about to unfold.

Soon after that vision, I received a text on the evening of Tuesday, January 7, from my friend's daughter, Brooke, who lives in Montana. "Are you near the fire?" her text read. Then came another text and a missed call from her brother, Nate.

At the moment, I was at the Walter Hoving Home, listening to my friend Connie lead a chapel service, so I quickly went to the restroom to call my neighbor Gilien. I was feeling increasingly nervous as she came on the other line and told me, "Yes, they are telling us to prepare to evacuate, but it's not mandatory."

My heart began to pound as I went back to the table where I had been sitting. I leaned toward my other friend Dottie and whispered into her ear, "There's a fire in Eaton Canyon, and I need to evacuate."

At first, she didn't understand what I was saying and asked me to repeat it. Once the gravity of the situation registered, she quickly texted her brother, who also lived in Altadena, very close to the foothills on Loma Alta.

I then rushed out of the building and down the stairs, my heart thumping loudly. The notorious Santa Ana winds were howling by now.

I need to get home, get my dog, and begin packing.

I turned the ignition to my car and peeled out of the parking lot with no time to lose.

Just then, my neighbor Emily called me as I was frantically driving up one street, then down another, trying to avoid a tree that had just fallen in the unruly winds.

"Tami," she told me, "I don't know where you are, but Noreen and I are packing up our things and evacuating."

At that moment, I realized I was driving down a one-way street—just like in a movie where everything seems to be going by in slow motion, and you're trying to tap into supernatural strength just to get to your destination. "It's going to be OK," I said to myself aloud. "There's only one car going south, and I will make a right-hand turn on the next block."

But as I turned onto Hill Avenue, I hit major traffic. It was a mass exodus of people fleeing the scene. There was also significant traffic heading north, but in my distressed state, I couldn't compute that the most effective way to get home would be to take side streets. It was as though we were all in the same boat, traumatized from the same event, trying to navigate our way home to rescue whatever we could.

As I was processing all of this—realizing that just thirty minutes before, I had no idea there was even a fire in Eaton Canyon—I decided to call Nate. In desperation I fervently began to relate, "Nate, please meet me at my house—I need to evacuate now!"

His response to me wasn't what I was expecting: "Well, I have plans tonight," he said calmly.

"What?!" I replied. "Nate, I will pay you! Please—I have to evacuate!"

He then let me know that he would call me back.

In utter shock and alarm, I cried out with an earnest prayer: "Lord, I need someone to help me. I can't do this alone!"

A few minutes later, Nate called me back. "I had no idea it was this bad," his voice said, now in a serious tone. "I will meet you at your house!"

I was eternally grateful to hear those words.

Once I approached the corner of New York and Hill Avenue, I came to the golf course, where it looked like there were flames all across the greens. I immediately thought, *OMG—the Altadena Golf Course is on fire!*

Only later did I learn that the mountainside was so brilliantly lit up in an orange glow that it appeared from my viewpoint—in total darkness—that the golf course was actually on fire. Other fire victims would share similar stories about how their perception of the fire was distorted because of the total blackout that night. Despite the initial illusion, the sad reality is that the Altadena Golf Course clubhouse did end up burning to the ground.

Next, I headed further northbound and was one mile from my house when I got a text warning. My phone vibrated with this message: *Warning! Mandatory evacuation in your area!*

I had just spoken to Gilien again and told her that Emily was packing up her things and evacuating. "What are you going to do?" I asked with all urgency.

She was very hesitant to say anything concrete, so I immediately followed up: "I'm going to my house to get my dog, pack up, and I'm going to evacuate."

"This has never happened before!" she replied.

"I know," I said, "but I'm heading to my house now—I'm just a mile away."

The entire neighborhood was blanketed in darkness. Not a single light could be seen except for the eerie glow of the fire on the mountainside. At this point, I noticed that there was a lot less traffic in my neighborhood, and I was relieved when I saw my street sign: "Highland Avenue… I'm almost home. Thank God!"

As I drove up the street, I could see my next-door neighbors pulling out of their driveway. "OK," I told myself, "I've got some time to grab Munchkins and pack up." Right when I turned into my driveway, there he was, wagging his tail, unaware of the fierce wildfire that was rapidly heading our way. I then grabbed a flashlight, brought him into the house, and collected all of his dog food, meds, and bowl, along with my meds. Without a minute to spare, I put them all on the kitchen table to throw into a bag later.

Next, I ran into my bedroom, grabbed my suitcase from the next room over, unzipped it, and began to throw clothes from my dresser into it. My rapid-fire thoughts told me: *I'll just seize the clothes that I wear most often—just pack for a week—then I can put them back in my dresser and closet in about a week when we return from the smoke damage.*

In the adrenaline rush of the moment, I was quickly packing my things when I heard Nate call out, "Hey Tama! I'm here!" He could tell I was frantic, and he knew what to do to put me at ease. "Don't worry," he said as he walked into the room, illuminated by flashlight. "Just tell me what to pack. It's going to be OK."

Nate then went through every room of the house, stripping down all framed family pictures and reminding me to take important documents. He even was careful to snatch up my laptop and chargers. There were so many things that I didn't think of because I was stressed to the max, but we went through each room together as Nate would ask me, "Is there anything else that you need? What about your hair dryer? Grab all essentials!"

I desperately fumbled for my phone, trying to contact Sharie, my housemate, to ask her what to pack, but to no avail. I went through each room, literally throwing things into the pocket of my jacket—a toothbrush, a phone holder, anything that was considered an essential.

Rapid questions burned in my mind: *Should I grab my mother's jewelry? Should I grab more things from the small room that we didn't pack? Should I look for my great-grandfather's LAPD officer's badge that my dad had kept as a family heirloom?* I quickly negotiated with myself, *I'm going to be back in about a week, so I don't need to grab those possessions.*

Turning to look in the small room, I decided in a split second to seize my dad's Army duffel bag of things that he had collected during his years serving in the military at the end of the Korean War, when he was deployed near the DMZ. For whatever reason, that bag was one of the most important things to me at that moment, as a symbol of my dad's legacy.

Suddenly, I heard a ringing sound, looked down at my phone, and noticed that Sharie was returning my phone call. *Thank God!* Sharie, who's a captain for the park rangers, had been deployed to help the firefighters who were fighting the wildfire in the Palisades.

"Sharie!" I exclaimed. "I've been trying to call you all evening. We have to evacuate! What do you want me to pack?"

"I'm so sorry," she replied. "I've been so busy helping with the Palisades Fire. Grab my three big boxes with my important documents in my bedroom."

"OK, what else?" I frantically replied. "I have your suitcase opened, and I can start packing your clothes!"

"It's OK—I'm on my way to the house, and I'll pack my clothes when I get there."

I was in utter disbelief but figured that Sharie, being a senior level park ranger, had more current updates regarding the extent of the Eaton Canyon Fire than I did. Unfortunately, Sharie never had a chance to return to pack her clothes or other belongings. Once she exited the 210 freeway at Arroyo Boulevard, there was so much traffic and the wind was blowing at such a furious speed that she decided to return to her friend's house. She had just personally witnessed the massive devastation, extreme heat, and flames of the Palisades Fire so she didn't want to deal with another wildfire that night. She surmised that our house wasn't that close to Eaton Canyon and that it wouldn't be considered in the fire zone anyways.

Still in the house, Nate and I grabbed her boxes and threw everything else into the car. I then paused for a moment, noticing that Munchkins was sitting on his light blue fleece blanket with his little, rubber reindeer toy in the passenger seat of my car. He looked happy and content, and it was at that moment that I knew it was time to go.

I carefully drove out my driveway, the wind howling in the utter darkness as I turned down my street—never to return to that beautiful Tudor house with the sage green trim, the house that had belonged to my family for decades and preserved so many wonderful memories.

It was the most surreal moment as we flew down Highland Avenue, followed by Nate's car. Though delirious and unable to think clearly, I instinctively knew not to drive down Hill, as there was an exodus of people, so we opted to go south on Lake. There we were confronted with major traffic.

"What should we do?" I asked Nate over the phone. "There's so much traffic on Lake—"

"We're going to take the side streets," he quickly replied. "Do you see Howard Street on your left? Take a left turn on Howard!"

"OK, sounds good—I never thought of taking side streets!" was my frantic reply.

"Have you never heard of 'Side-street Sally'?" Nate said with a laugh.

It felt good to laugh in the midst of the sheer adrenaline and chaos after trying to desperately pack in total darkness. I shot up a quick prayer, "Thank You, Lord, for Nate! I never would have been able to do this without his help!"

That night I stayed with a friend in Pasadena whose house was outside the evacuation zone. Exhausted, my head hit the pillow in near-instant sleep.

Experiencing a wildfire is unlike anything I have ever dealt with before. I was confronted with the trauma of the event, but yet I am so grateful for the smallest gifts. This unenviable experience truly has given me a different perspective on life. There have been so many silver lining moments—from extreme generosity of financial support to my cousins Sherri and Dean Edwards, who so graciously invited Munchkins and me into their home to live, to the prayers of countless others.

The aftermath of the Eaton Fire set a new chapter in motion, where I have been swamped with so many decisions to make, simply to regain some semblance of normalcy. Even so, I'm so thankful for the wonderful and encouraging support from my neighbors. This wildfire was unlike any other—a total blackout with winds clocking in at 100 miles per hour that knocked down entire trees, telephone lines, and even stop lights that just lay motionless on the pavement.

I would find out later that my neighbor Suzie and her husband, who lived just north of me, chose not to evacuate because the wind had shifted west. So, at 11 p.m. that night, they decided to go to bed, since after all, in the decades that we lived on this street, we'd never had to evacuate from a wildfire. It wasn't until 1:30 a.m. that they were startled awake to find their house on fire! The flames were rapidly spreading to Kate's house next door, but gratefully, they were able to get out safely by 2 a.m.

The winds that night were unforgiving, as the embers ferociously flying through the air lit up their tall pine tree like a roman candle. The red-hot embers then skipped two houses and landed on the large oak tree branches that enveloped the roof of my house. This took place at about 2:30 a.m. on the morning of Wednesday, January 8.

I decided to go to work that Wednesday, after my friend told me that she had heard that the firefighters should have control of the wildfire by early morning. It was around 10:35 a.m. when I received a text from Emily: "I'm sorry to tell you, Tami, but your house didn't make it."

What?! I screamed in my head. I quickly notified my coordinator, who then took over my classroom as I dashed out the front door of my school to call Emily. I *needed* to clarify what her text actually meant. My body was shaking as I approached my car and quickly rang her number.

"Emily, did you visit your house this morning?"

"Yes," she replied. "I'm so sorry, Tami—your house didn't make it. Our house is still standing."

Those words burned in my chest. *How is that possible? We have never had a wildfire that has come that close in over 50 years!*

My wounded heart sank so deep, and I was unable to process what she had just told me. After all, this was the house that I grew up in—the house that my grandparents had bought in 1945 at the end of World War II. Now there was another war to fight, a personal one to overcome, on an entirely different field of battle.

In the midst of the wildfire's devastating wake, my neighbors on Highland Avenue came together in the most amazing ways, and I am forever grateful for them and all of their support. Since this was the house of my childhood years, I have known some of my neighbors for more than 30 years. We share wonderful memories of beautifully decorated neighborhood block parties that initiated as a modest picnic twenty-five years ago. Kate created the event to look like a Hollywood set design with music, delicious food, and drinks. My parents were always in attendance, and every year, my dad would wholeheartedly join in as "set up crew," as it literally took two days to create this amazing masterpiece.

During those first few crucial months of 2025, we would have our weekend neighborhood Zoom call and aptly created four various committees: security, rebuilding, law and litigation, and social. We also established a Highland Google email group and spreadsheet listing everything from recommended architects and contractors to electricians and plumbers.

We have already had several gatherings at various restaurants, the Huntington Library and Botanical Gardens, and we are currently planning our next neighborhood block party for October 2025. Our block party this year will be different; a majority of the original decorations were unfortunately burned in the wildfire, and only the light poles survived. Nevertheless, we will gather once again this time on the south side of our street, where seventeen homes are still monumentally standing today as a prophetic picture that not all was lost in the devastating Eaton Canyon wildfire.

A few months ago, we were picking up the broken pieces of our homes, searching for our cherished possessions. I had heard about Franklin Graham's ministry called "Samaritan's Purse" and made an appointment with them, knowing that I wouldn't be able to sift through the remaining contents from the fire without assistance.

So, on February 8, we all gathered in front of my house, adorned in white disposable coveralls with bright orange shirts that read, "Samaritan's Purse—Helping in Jesus' Name." I became very emotional realizing that not only did ten strangers show up to help me sift through the ashes, but it was exactly one month to the day of the devastating wildfire that had destroyed my home. For whatever reason, the exterior walls of the house were still standing, which had effectively insulated a burning inferno inside—leading to the point where the remaining contents were unrecognizable.

In this sacred moment, I asked the leader if I could pray before we began. He agreed, and everyone gathered in a circle, holding hands as I thanked God for His mercy and surrendered to Him whatever we would recover that day.

Then, after four hours of sifting and digging, we were able to recover my great-grandfather's LAPD police badge, melted from the tremendous heat, and some china that had belonged to my mom. But what miraculously survived as a prophetic sign were three untouched Lladro angel figurines that my dad had given to my mom for her birthday. Most of the dishes and cups had been shattered to pieces and melted from the intensity of the fire—with the exception of these three exquisite angels. They were a heavenly gift. It was almost as though God was telling me at that very moment, *"I'm watching over you, and I've not forgotten you!"*

Cliff, the leader of the group, then shared with me how encouraged he was by my prayers and positive, hopeful demeanor amidst this unbelievable tragedy. He shared that they had encountered some unkind, unappreciative residents in the last several weeks and that my house was his last assignment before he flew back to Seattle.

I, for my part, had been so encouraged by them and their willingness to help me, and yet I was encouraging and blessing them as well! It's amazing how God works in mysterious ways and knows just what we need in the midst of devastation and tremendous loss.

There are so many divine appointments that I've had in the last several months, but one that I truly cherish—and that was clearly orchestrated by God—was the exchange I had with my gardener's son, Robert. As a contractor, Robert shared with me that he lived on the west side of Lake Avenue and had lost both his house and his garage where all of his tools were stored.

Well, Nate and I had been rummaging through my garage that was miraculously still standing after the fires, getting rid of several items, when Nate told me, "You should give your dad's Shopsmith to Robert!"

For the last eight years, I had been trying to sell this monstrous five-in-one woodworking system that came complete with five other boxes, but to no avail. It had taken up a large part of the garage, equivalent to a small Fiat. My dad, beside himself, had brought it home one day, unbeknownst to my mom.

"What is that? And how much did it cost?" my mom inquired once she noticed the elephant in the room.

"It's a Shopsmith," he replied. "I can make all kinds of things with it!"

My dad was overjoyed that he had brought home this behemoth of a woodworking saw so that he could build furniture for Josh, but my mom was less than pleased. Thus was the situation that had claimed so much garage space for the better half of a decade. So, Nate's suggestion to gift it to Robert provided a solution that was both timely and a long time coming!

The next week, Robert came by to pick up this massive tool. As he was loading it onto his truck, he said to me, *"This is going to help rebuild Altadena!"*

My heart was so thankful in that moment. God knew all along who would need that Shopsmith the most, and I'm so grateful that, despite everything that Robert lost, I was able to bless him with it.

Another aspect of gratitude that has enlivened my heart for these past several months is the knowledge that my parents never had to experience a wildfire evacuation in their lifetime. It would have been devastating for them to witness firsthand the massive devastation and damage that was left behind in the wake of one of the most horrific wildfires in California.

The embers have left behind so much heartache—there is so much that we will never recover. Yet, at the same time, my heart remains grateful, and my memories are still preserved that no wildfire will ever burn away.

ABOUT THE AUTHOR

Tamara Lennon is a dedicated elementary teacher with a passion for serving her community and encouraging others through compassion. A mother, survivor, and woman of unshakable faith, Tamara has walked through the darkest valleys and emerged with a message of hope. Whether in the classroom, in her neighborhood, or on the page, she seeks to be a messenger of hope and healing for the brokenhearted.

She is currently in the process of rebuilding her home after the wildfires and is in the final phase with the architect and structural engineer. The aftermath of the wildfires has taught her many lessons of hope and resilience. She is grateful to her family, friends, and neighbors on Highland who have supported and encouraged her through this next chapter unfolding in her life.

Hiking Out of the Wilderness is Tamara's first book. She lives with her beloved dog, Munchkins, in Southern California.